Seasons

A Collection of Poetry and Prose

Sasha Garcia

to my son,
light of my world,
joy of my life.

& to the love that
showed me to
always reach for
something bigger,
you will always
have a piece of me.

penetrate.

penetrate my bones with the love you promised me
even though broken promises oozed from your
pores with lies
every time you looked at me
i forgave you

tsunami of your love.

i want to write poetry on your lips
i don't think i've told you that yet
to sink the words into the very flesh of you
line after line
verse after verse
to get caught in you
wrapped in you
intertwining my legs
for you to taste the stanzas
of love that flow through me

build.

i want to build castles with you
built from the love that erupts from the very depths of my soul
capturing the essence of me
you don't realize the love that courses through my veins
it's deeper than the oceans that beings have drowned in
you are the warmth to my earth

lies.

i find myself sleep walking through centuries of
broken love
by lovers with broken promises etched into their
spine
etched into their hands
while they touched me
i thought i'd lose my mind
touching their flesh gave me a high
and when it finally came down
i could recite poetry in their lies

wear your name.

my mind dances with thoughts
tip toeing with your name on my tongue
goosebumps create indentations of your skin
please listen when i tell you
my love lines wear your name so effortlessly

commute.

empty trains
busy commute
my mind runs a mile a minute
in hopes to figure out exactly why i feel the way that i do
the highs seem high
but the lows?
they have me crawl on hands and knees
blood pouring from my palms
because of all the glass that has embedded in my skin
it leaves scars
from past lovers
lovers that discarded the very love that they begged for
see my love seemed as though it was enough, for a moment
they drowned in the very thought of me
soaking me up
the inspiration that seeped from my pores until i became nothing
and nothing became an empty train on busy commutes
with my mind running a mile a minute
trying to figure out why i feel the way that i do

you.

your essence has found ways into my skin
and when you're no longer close to me
i crave you

last breath.

stop letting me love you like this
i cant breathe because i’ve been breathing into you
suffocating myself so you could breathe
wait
i’m not ready to stop
because id die
die giving you my last breath

move me.

love move me
like unearthing flowers to water them
in the home of your love
let the butterflies in my stomach release
so that you can see how beautiful they are,
while trying to count how many you've given me
since i first laid eyes on you
love move me
earth shattering
body trembles
move me in ways i yearn for you
i thirst for you
in ways that leave me famished
hungry for the very thought of you

before the sun comes up.

alarm rings
my body found its way to the other side of the bed
i stretch and shiver because of the cold
almost forgetting your body was what kept me
warm last night
my body melts, immediately you feel like home
and i realize
i wouldn't mind doing this for the rest of my life

sacrifice.

you left her
but i still smell her on your skin
how does that make me feel any better?
i don't want pieces of you
you have become the epitome of heartbreak
my heart palpitates when you're near me
the moment i know you're with her
it stops
insecurity engulfs me
i want to be enough
i don't feel enough
you suck me into your whirlwind of love and i am
stuck
spinning in a web of pain
you hurt me so you won't hurt her
how did i become the sacrifice?

lies part 2.

i can trace the crevices of your lies
in the cracks of your lips
my honey can't soothe them any longer

over.

and why is it that my heart can't seem to fathom
what it would be like to lose you?
because losing myself costs so much more

secrets.

secretly i crave the intimacy
that radiates off of other lovers

heart.

wonder what you'd feel like if i walked away
with your heart in my hand?
exactly
what you have done to me

april 19th, 2019.

selfishly i want to keep you.
because i know when i walk away
i'll miss your warmth
i'll miss your touch
i'll miss your kiss
but i think i've already missed these parts of us
but i have to let you go
for my own sanity
because i've been losing sleep over you
and it's been driving me crazy

you see i've dedicated a special
monument in my heart for you
and i suffer in silence as you go about your days
loving freely
and i'm tired
my love craves the love it gives
and here i am
silently screaming in a room filled with people my
love for you
and you stand right next to me
not even turning around
so i have to let you go
for my own sanity
because losing myself in you
isn't even worth it.

fire and earth.

she was fire,
that destroyed everything in her path
i am earth
and here is where she felt the warmth
of the earth through her destruction
and they said we weren't even supposed to coincide

mornings.

i want to see the sun rise on your sleeping face
while i watch your chest rise and fall
letting my fingers gently caress your face so i don't
wake you
and if you'd awake for just a moment
i'd kiss your lips
i guess this just means
i couldn't see a morning where you weren't there

exhaustion.

i'm exhausted
exhausted from stretching myself thin
for lovers who don't reciprocate the same
sleep walking through centuries of broken love
by lovers with broken promises etched into their
spine
etched into their hands
while they touched me
i thought i'd lose my mind
touching their flesh gave me a high
that when it finally came down
i could recite their lies in poetry

vulnerable.

i wonder how easily the lies slip from your tongue
and how easily my heart falls into every
single
one

broken bones.

her words broke bones
while they healed
i licked my own wounds
i need love too
but you gave it away so freely
the fingers that gripped my neck to silence me
were the same ones that held my hand in crowded rooms
so everyone knew that i was yours

lifetimes.

i’ve seen you in a vision
face unseen
but your scent lingers always
your touch reminds me of what home feels like
you’ve been mine in a few lifetimes
i’ve contemplated on what if’s for far too long
i journey through your eyes
trying to find what makes fucking sense
but baby nothing makes sense and
i just want to make love to you until the next red
moon
and when it comes again
i want to make love into lifetimes with you

riot.

my loves a riot
it shakes kings from their thrones
they sit so high upon
and only one deserves it
that one
will shake me to the core
calming the chaos
that seeps from my bones

february.

your flesh against mine
i can feel your heart pulse in between my legs
with your tongue invading every crevice of my body
that makes me forget where i am
who i am
that i even exist
forget my name
forget that my body will not float on the clouds
you've given me once you walked away
once you've run away
i capture this moment in memories
imbedded into my skin
because baby you taught me one thing
when the clouds fade
the sun always shines
even when you're not here

thinking of you in the winter.

i want to do what the sun does to you in the
summer time
when it warms your skin
or when april showers catch you mid walk to the
train
surprising you
but your face glistens

distance.

i hope you find a love that lingers on your skin
no matter the distance

december.

and just like that you have me
your voice will echo in my head
and stay embedded there
following me through days
when i can’t feel you next to me
it sends chills down my spine
and the goosebumps that go through
every layer of my skin
ill be your canvas as long
as your voice will always linger

universe.

the way she looks at me
it’s like she sees the universe inside of me

next lifetime.

let me heal you
take the pain that rises through your skin
because no one has known what to do with it
suck it from your pores
take your pain into mine
i'll die for it
if it meant loving you in this lifetime
and the next

sweet november.

"you're an inspiration"
spilled from her lips
and immediately my heart flutters
if only she knew just a few months ago
i couldn't even look myself in the mirror
and now the mirrors look for me
inspiration bleeds through her words
and i am finding that my words are
sometimes lost in her eyes
and damn if that doesn't feel good

beg.

beg.
give me you.
beg
so that i can engulf you
beg
so you just know how much i need you
please don't make me beg
because i'd get on my knees right now
beg
for your love
watch as the strangers watch
the desperation that pains my face as i beg
i need your lips against my skin to make me feel
alive
because baby you don't even know
that you light a fire that feels like home

stuck.

stuck
between fighting myself to love you
stuck with not just ripping my heart
from my very chest
as the blood escapes
as my face turns pale from losing it all
but smiling because it was all worth it
you're dangerous
but damn it if i can't help
but intertwine myself into you
leave your essence in my very skin
so i can carry you everywhere always
in all ways

dear lover.

i leave my vulnerability in the room
where our secrets are held
i wondered if you ever really paid attention
to how i throw on my mask before leaving for the
day
and by the end of the day
my body wears shame well
my shoulders a little heavier
my stride slow
making sure i am balanced before i break
dear lover
wrap your arms around me during the days
i don't speak when i walk through the door
for i know my cries will be muffled by the shower
and you won't see them through the scorching
steam
i hide my pain well
but the moment you embrace me
i break
my breaths are shallow
tears stream
with you i don't need to always be strong
with you
i can be seen
with you,
well
dear lover
here's my blueprint to love
to loving me

nourshing.

let me be the blood that runs through your veins
but doesn't kill you
if i leave from this earth
but nourishes your growth
let me infuse myself into your spine
so that you know i'll never leave you
when the world tries to break you
a healthy addiction that allows flowers to grow
from the very palms of your hands
let me show you that love exists
hold my hand while warmth exudes through our
bodies
love exists baby let me show you

scars.

i wear my scars well
deeply imbedded into my bones
so no one can see just how many have been broken

erase.

erasing you from my physical
seemed easy
erasing you from my mind
became the hardest task
memories bled through the sheets when i lay awake
at night
scents bring me back to moments with you
i feel you when i don't want too
writing poetry on the walls in my room
because i just couldn't find space in my head

blueprint.

i was told one that i was "too much"
that my love was too much
that if my hands lingered to long on her hand
it disgusted her
like her capacity to "love" were insults
insults that imbedded into my soul
i fought with my mind
because i couldn't look into the mirror
on the outside i'd wear "wife" well
on the inside i died, every time she touched me
without my permission
screams penetrated, stuck at the base of my throat
and when she wasn't looking my way
tears would fall down the very cheeks
she would grab to shut me up
i prayed for strength
to gain heart where i had lost it all
to breathe where my breath was my own
and not intertwined with hers
her words broke bones,
and i licked my own wounds
i painted my pain with the blood from my wrists
when she wasn't looking
begging for someone to hear me
see, i only wanted love
a love that could stand storms and
would be patient enough to wait for the calm
here is the blueprint to my love after the pain
i require love that drenches deserts
where my hand lingers longer
just to feel your skin close to mine
i desire a love that holds accountability,
that heals when i thought i was broken

the mirrors looked shattered every time i looked at
them
then i realized, the only reason why they looked
shattered
was because i looked at them through eyes full of
tears
but here i am staring at the same mirror
with love and i found myself
those silenced screams, have been written through
poetry
here's to painting my pain through words,
and sharing the blueprint to my love

nightmare.

my mind constantly plays tricks on me
like a carousel in a nightmare
i cannot wake up from
with that i find myself rummaging through the darkness
the earth's warmth beneath my feet
my hands touching the branches that are ahead of me
i hear you but i wonder if those are just the voices telling me
i can’t reach you
the walk smells of lavender
calming each nerve ending in my body
i feel relaxed
this nightmare seems like it’s ending
until i touch you
reaching through the thick of the trees
and you disappear
forcing this nightmare to become a reality

intimacy.

secretly i crave you
to crave what the words feel like when you take
paper to pen
to be kissed by the very mouth that has spoken to
souls
i crave the intimacy of silence with you
to listen to the earth change seasons
and watch the green of the leaves turn golden

blood and bones.

i envy your wildness
and how free you are in the jungle
everyone loves a wild one
even the quiet ones
that you pull from their darkness
but leave thirsty for more
once you're finished with them

i used to be the quiet one that you tossed to the side
but my body wouldn't allow me
to be detained to a slumber of sorrow
crying in the darkest of hours
by morning wiping the tears that left marks on my
cheeks

i committed myself to you not seeing them
i wondered if you even looked twice
your wildness left trails of ruined lovers
bones of their corpses that imbedded
love from their marrow
everyone loves a wild one
until there's nothing left of themselves
but blood and bones

needle.

take me there.
to where the addiction that consumed you,
consumes me
but wait
it has
i kept dreaming of this eternity with you
that i could never get
so settle for those vibes you could
only give me for a moment
addicting
addiction
like a needle in the vein
i waited for you to pierce me with every drug
that allowed me to see you
even in the darkest of rooms

senses.

i'd do it again.
i'd relive the moment just so you could recite
poetry in-between my legs
where laughter filled the room for a few seconds
making sure the neighbors didn't hear
the pleasure you gave me
i'd do it again
just to feel your hands touch my body
or the way you looked at me
i'd do it again
if you asked that of me
but is that foolish of me?
possibly
but i just want to our fingers to interlock one last
time
before my next life

september.

the sun rose
i had to peel my body off of yours
your skin against mine feels like home
you grabbed me before i could crawl out of bed
without you noticing
i nuzzled my head between your neck
kissing you
a smile spreading across your face
made me envy you
made me envy your skin
giving you the love
lovers didn't know how to give
i whisper these things, hoping that you hear
as i try and get ready for the day
i watch you sleep in envy
because i know that i am not the only one loving
you
but i'm not jealous right now
because my bed is occupied by your body
even for a moment

flowers.

did i tell you my ribs cracked open when i tried to
love you?
i forgive you,
to allow these flowers to bloom from
the broken bones of my opened chest
which refused to grow because
i couldn't forgive you
i didn't do this for you
i did this for me

october.

if i could crawl into bed with you right now
while your arms wrap around my tired body
i feel like i’d be in heaven
intimacy with kisses from you placed on my third
eye
while you explore the very depths of my being
through words

attention to detail.

i could see lifetimes in the lines of your fingers
and your lips tell stories my heart wants to hear
attentive
attention
to the simplest details of your eyes scanning
over my body as though
you want to devour
every
single
inch
of me

drunk.

i want to indulge in you
drink me until you overflow

unravel.

unravel me
unwrap me
unearth the bruised memories that have made me
who i am
so you can understand
why the weight of the world ran along my spine
and if it broke
i'd lose my footing
nurture me
kiss every inch of my soul
for it will allow me to feel you

coffee.

i had coffee this morning and thought about you
as my lip stained the ceramic glass
i thought about my lips against your bare neck
leaving it's mark so everyone knows that a poet was
here
tracing my tongue with poetry
my legs clenched as i thought about
your hands caressing my inner thigh
coffee spilled
waking me from my daydream
and it left me wet with the thought of you

sweet.

your lips tasted of honey
i didn't get tired of tasting

lose.

you lose her when you find excuses to not make her smile
you lose her when your arms don't wrap around her when the tears fall
you lose her when you don't make her feel secure
you lose her, when you show her you don't love her
you lose her when she starts being invisible to you

not welcomed here.

i didn't invite him into
my young body
leaving scars that only i have been able to find
he was never welcomed in my home

intellect.

you leave me speechless
grasping at the air to find words
after you drench my panties and rip them off
after you seep into the delicate crevices of my mind
no one could reach

fire.

it’s something that you do
that makes my body quiver at your touch
your words find their way
around the barriers of my heart
to be in your presence
sets my soul on fire

earth.

you woke something in me that
devoured a hunger in my soul
my body warm with passion
warm with an earthly touch
you could only dream of
i pulled up the ground so you can feel like home
i turned empty spaces into ponds filled with lillies
and named each one after you
i planted trees that we could sit under in years to
come
but i was too much
you were too much
we were too much
so i'll touch you with a passion that wakens
something in your soul
so you'll never forget me.
because you'll never forget me,
even if you tried

blame game.

you gave me everything
so that i could breathe again
so i could pick up these shattered pieces of love
that only existed in fantasies
used you?
you willingly gave your soul to the devil
and blamed me
now you lie in the poetry that seeps into the pores
that make others drown in it

you.

writing about you doesn't even feel the same.

selfish.

if i knew how hard loving you would be
i would've saved it for myself

may flowers.

they said april showers brought may flowers
but i left room for april to bring tears to my eyes
and may broke me

trauma.

what ripped through my skin
like a reminder that no one could see

letting you go.

i learned to love myself more once i let you go.

coffee shops.

a place that i can escape to
to try and find you through crowds of people
while enjoying my cup of the day
if I close my eyes hard enough
i'll be reminded of what you taste like

museums.

i found a flyer of a museum we visited together
tucked into the spine of a poetry book
the irony
i opened the book
cracked the spine
while you cracked mine
and left me to tend to my own wounds

texas.

anticipating your call
your smile at the end of that receiver
your lips parting to speak my name
i'd be crazy if i didn't tell you
how my smile radiates a room when you're
mentioned
or how my heart skips just a few beats when my
phone rings
and it's you on the other side
i'm just trying to show you what life would look
like if loving you was in the deck of cards
we draw when trying to read the lines our hands
have
made through weathered storms
i want to write poetry in between the cracks of your
heart
you've been trying to conceal
because baby there's an art to my loving
an art to making your smile create memories
etched into my mind
and i'm just trying to make
you a canvas to my love
if you let me.

come home.

the lover.
the lover that begs for me to come home
it does something to me
it brings my aching bones to rest
crawling to you after being defeated
the lover knows
knows that every step feels like eternity
eternity i searched years to look for
and you were standing right there
in front of me
come home
my body jolts
exhaustion finds it way into my veins
and my love drains
love is my first language
and when i found my skin pressed against yours
after searching through hell to rescue you from sin
i whispered to you
come home.

bookshelf.

you took me off a shelf of books
dusted me off and reminded me of my potential
reminded me of the queen that i am
reminded me that i have unfinished chapters that
laid dormant with unfinished poetry that could
rewrite history
to leave a legacy.
the spine of my book warm in your hands
reminded you that no matter how many times i am
shelved, the fire runs deep.
engulfing you into my world
to bring out the writer that burns in you.

fountain of youth.

your words resonated with me
they took me to a memory
where i found myself in between your thighs
drinking from your fountain
for a moment escaping reality
wrapped in the fantasy of you
i remember waking up
you across the room,
smoking a cigarette,
blowing the smoke out the window.
and all i could remember was
maybe i did this in another lifetime
love you like this, effortlessly
and without a care in the world.

aching bones.

distance makes it okay to be distant
but facetimes make me want to be closer to you
to know what your lips feel like against my skin
or how warm your embrace could be
burning desire to have your voice open my sine
with your words
a longing that's starting to make
my bones ache

seconds.

my mind is doing dance numbers
wanting to know what your arms feel like wrapped around me
what your lips taste like
what it's like to feel your warmth against my skin
anticipating the days
counting down the seconds
and damn i wondered if i close my eyes hard enough
you'd be standing right in front of me

home.

she said “get out of my head”
i told her i’m just tryna live in it
find a seat in your mental
making it home to love

painful beauty.

i want to exist in you
embed my love into your bones
baby, there's almost always
beauty in the pain.

faded.

flashbacks
leave me breathless
leave me saddened by the memories
we shared and if they were even real
we spent three seasons together
fall, winter and spring
and by spring time
i was dying on the inside
wilting flowers in my chest
that wouldn't grow until i let you go
i remember the small things
your hand on my back so
i wouldn't sway with the
movement of the train
or how i used to watch you write
poetry right next to me
memories
became faded
only ignited by a moving train
or the smell of you with someone
that wore the same thing
but here's two three seasons spent together
because you'll never get me back

fragile.

i want to experience you
i want to explore you
become enamored by your every thought
i want to climb
no i want to
crawl into the spaces no one was willing to go
through to understand
exactly who you are
i want to get my hands dirty
i want to unearth your garden
plant my seeds there
to show you what growth looks like
to show you how love exists
even in the dirt that no one looks twice at
and baby i'm just trying to drown in you
inhale you
exist in you
i promise
i'll handle you with care

fire.

heat flushed my cheeks at the mention of your
name
palms sweating from nerves that engulf my entire
body
and baby if you could feel my heart
i think it could shake mountains
to exude love would be an understatement
i want to bathe in it
watch your body convulse from my love
to be your remedy
your antidote
to this addiction called our love

here's my heart, take it.

my heart skipped a beat
like if i could literally pull it out of my chest
you could feel how it beat for you
how i breathed for you
and baby here just take it
because i know it would be safe in the softness of
your grasp
here take it
i know that my love embodies the heart
encompassing each part of my body
for yours to keep
so baby here
just take it
it's yours
i'm yours
til the end
for lifetimes
after

levitate.

levitate in love
allow me to help you reach peaks of your mind
you've been too stubborn to reach
to allow you to feel
everything
anything
in each waking moment
to be touched by the essence of me
you call it brujeria
well i call it love in its purest form
not everyone has even touched that level yet
not everyone was warranted this type of love
yet this type of love is all i have to offer you
levitate in love
let me help you reach peaks of your mind
even when i can't touch you physically

loving you.

you embody the love that i've longed for
in your vessel i see the soul that i've loved
in so many lives before now
you speak to my heart in whispers
igniting fires in me
speaking life into the core of me
we belong together can not even put into words
of how i was molded to love you
how you've inspired the pen to the paper
i would be crazy not to embrace you in your entirety
to heal wounds that you can no longer see
to love your raw and pure heart
to cultivate lands in your garden
with permanent residence
i may not have a green thumb
but loving you has been so easy
falling for you so easy
that i've built flower beds in our broken bones
for all they required was love
and how that flows so effortlessly
i found peace in you even with the chaos
that tried to strip what little of life i thought i had
left
you breathe life into me
into a love that could stir commotions in peaceful
riots

oh mother.

i’m triggered
by the way you can so easily toss me to the side
as though you did not nurture me in a womb
that you carried for 9 months
how easily i’m dismissed
but you nourished me inside you
do you call that love?
i call that absence
and for so long i tried to find love
in other beings because there was a lack there of
triggered
relationships turned spoiled
friendships tarnished
because i didn’t even know what love meant
until loving myself
meant slowly losing the woman
who gave birth to me

when it rains in new york.

today
today i felt the beads of sweat form on my forehead
today i find myself catching my breath twice
not because of the humidity that new york has
graced us with
but because of the anxiety that crawled up my
throat
and if i heard one more piece of news that
took away a little of peace
i'd break
my throat held stories
it held pain that broke me in ways my lungs
collapsed
over
and
over
again
and it held tears that the deserts
would be jealous of if they came down
today i was jealous of the peace
that i needed because it was tucked away
in the little bit of hope i place hidden in my ribs
keeping my lungs in place so i wouldn't collapse

library.

my fingers float over books in a lover's library
yours so quiet
but radiated an energy i couldn't explain
even if i wanted
my hand touched you three times
gently picking you up
placing my hand on your spine to support the weight
worn with use
my heart pained
opening the cover of you
you moaned
as if every vertebrae in your spine
calcified every ligament in your chapters
with time, infusing each one.
no one knew what to do so i held you steady
watered the crevices of each page with my love
and watched as you submerged yourself in it
the love reviving you

bruised.

apologies spewed from your lips like the lies that
came after
and all i could do to hide the pain
was grab my makeup to blend the bruises with my
skin
but eventually it would wash away
and i'd be left looking at whoever i became in the
mirror

remember when my heart shook?

i remember when i first met you
i remember how nervous i was
how i hoped you didn't hear my heartbeat through
my chest
i remember the first time i told you i was battered
and bruised
and the marks that were on my body started to melt
away by your love
i remember when you told me you loved me
i hesitated
not because i didn't love you back but because who
could love a broken...
who could love the broken me
i remember the first time you kissed me
the world stopped
and if i could carry that moment in a mason jar
and keep it in my back pocket, i would
i never thought that i was unable to receive love
i just thought that i was only able to give it and one
day
maybe one day
i'd die just knowing i had loved, even if i didn't get
it back.
that would be my ticket to heaven right?
i remember the day that my heart fell into the
palms of your hands
you gently placed it into your chest
and told me "i got you"
baby if i died in that moment,
my ticket to heaven would be finally loving
someone
that loved me back.

whispers.

the lover
the lover that begs for me to come home
it does something to me
it brings my aching bones to rest
crawling to you after being defeated
the lover knows
knows that every step feels like eternity
eternity i searched years to look for
and you were standing right there
in front of me
come home
my body jolts
exhaustion finds it way into my veins
and my love drains
love is my first language
and when i found my skin pressed against yours
after searching through hell to rescue you from sin
i whispered to you
come home

pressure.

pressure
the feeling that weighs heavily on my chest
it makes it hard to breathe
break hearts?
never my intention
but here i am breaking mine over again
with every crack of my rib it gets harder to explain
the pain
that radiates through my chest
i go into shock
my face contorted in pain
screams won't find their way out of my mouth
i struggle through shallow breaths
just to tell you i love you
and i love you seems so damn far away
break hearts?
never my intention
but here i am breaking mines over again
just to write poetry in the crevices of your heart
but there's never been any room for me
so i had to release you
to allow these flowers to bloom
from the cracks of my opened chest

blind.

i blindly walk through days
hoping no one sees me
hoping that i could move through the crowds
without anyone noticing the weight that clings to
my ankles
that bounds my hands together
that grips my throat
it leaves me silenced
you expect the writer to spew love poems from
veins that have dried up
blood soaked tears on unfilled notebooks
i'm tired
can't you see?
sometimes the earthly woman in me
needs water to be drenched down every part of my
body
just to get another glimpse of what love feels like

cradle you.

i want to bask in the infinite love you spew when you speak my name
i want to ease the pain that aches in your bones
settling there while you move through your days
hoping no one stops for conversation to see your aching
i want to cradle you
to show you that love exists
to kiss the tears that no one has been able to see
because they haven't been looking hard enough

nightmares.

cold sweats.
drench with nightmares at the base of my neck.
clenched fists leave nail indentations,
blood screaming to release from my palms
i'm exhausted
my breath has left my lungs
body tensed from nerves
lips quiver from the tears that have managed to
fall down my cheeks
i reach for you
to rescue me from the tremors in my fingers
your warmth is still there
but you're not
i crawl to your side of the bed
inhale your scent to settle me
close my eyes
and dream in a world that takes me
the cycle continues

i love you.

you speak life into a body where at some point
i couldn’t even breathe without gasping for air

uninvited.

i remember when you used to try and climb inside
my walls
without permission and i'd die
over
and
over
again

broken bones.

i’ve had to rearrange the bones in my rib cage
to make room for love that should’ve never existed

missed connection.

i keep imaging what love would've looked like
at the right moment
that moment that everyone says exist
but really doesn't
the right moment for our love

time.

i tried to find patience in the waiting game
of your love.

rearrange.

you pull love out of my rib cage
rearranged my organs to place pieces of you
in hidden crevices of my body cavity

so how am i not supposed to love you?

reassurance.

your words pacify the hurt just a little
my anxiety subsides and it doesn't feel like my ribs
are cracking
and my heart is seemingly intact
i caught my breath and watched as every ache in my
body fell
i wondered
i wondered if you felt that when i gave you the little
bit
of reassurance to end your curiosity
if you loving me was enough.

truth is.

i felt you slip through my fingers as you walked
away from me
with each step my heart was ripped from my chest
and if loving you would hurt this much
i keep telling myself i wouldn't want this
but maybe for a moment just to be in your arms
again.

intentions.

i tried to mend the broken pieces in you
while breaking myself every damn time.

symphony.

i want to orchestrate a symphony on the curve of
your back
i don't think you heard me
i want to orchestrate a symphony on the curve of
your back
i want to pull the very strings of you
and watch as my fingers recite poetry on each
vertebrate
i want to infuse my words in every broken bone
you've arranged for people who only wanted to
break you
and with that,
the love i have will shake the very core of you

wrong timing.

i remember the way your lips felt against mine
how my body slightly shivered from your touch
how nervous i was the first time we made love
i remember i enjoyed waking up to your embrace
and the smell of your skin
i remember thinking i could do this forever
i remember the first time you told me you love me
and how i begged if you'd just let me love you back
i remember your smile
and how i wanted capture it in every photograph
just so i'd always know how happy you were
i remember your warmth and how your body
was always hotter than mine no matter the
temperature
i remember the first time we met
and the butterflies that swam in the pit of my
stomach
i remember when our time was over
and you'd had to leave me id ache inside
i remember the tears i'd cry while you weren't
looking
your memory so vivid in my head

when you left me my heart didn't have enough
time to catch up with my mind
your scent lingered in the bed we shared

i was only left with memories that bombarded my
daily thoughts
you were deeply intertwined in the everyday
and i didn't know how to let you go
text messages unanswered
calls diminished over time

i miss you's less frequent

i love you's nonexistent
and all i could remember was begging you
if you'd just let me love you back
instead i'll just sit with the photographs of your
smile
and remember how happy you were

maybe you'll come back because i still love you
and i don't want to just remember anymore

rewind.

i'd beg your shadow to stay with me
while you walked away

muse.

i've craved your intimacy
so, I wrote poetry in your absence

pause.

i don’t know what it means not to have you speak
life into my poetry
stuck in this feeling I don’t know how to get out of
because loving you was easy
but letting go has been so damn hard

the walk.

i created room for you to bleed your love
into my veins and watch you walk
away with my heart

kismet.

do you how many lifetimes i’ve loved you?

Sasha Garcia

is a puerto rican poet
from brooklyn, ny.
she finds inspiration through
love and heartbreak.
every poem has a muse that
entices you into her world.
she brings every feeling
you've felt through words.
a dream she's
always possessed.
here she shares the
pieces of her with you.

....until we meet again.

www.ingramcontent.com/pod-product-compliance
Ingram Content Group UK Ltd.
Pitfield, Milton Keynes, MK11 3LW, UK
UKHW042014190726
13854UKWH00005B/2280